The Real Magic of Santa Claus

Honest Answers
That Will Make You Believe

Anthony N. Canamucio

Printed in the United States of America

ISBN# 1449538363
EAN-13# 9781449538361

To Gabriela, Alexa, Amanda and Andrew.
May your lives always be filled with magic.

Is Santa Claus Real?

If someone gave you this book, it is probably because you are asking this question. I am going to help you know for sure, though I must warn you, it will not be the yes or no answer you are looking for.

As you get older, you begin to question things. This is good—it is how you learn.

How old is Santa? Is it really possible to visit every house in the world in just one night? How can one sleigh hold so many gifts? How about these questions: Can reindeer really fly? How can such a chubby guy fit down a chimney? Don't all of those cookies and milk give him an upset stomach? How can he know who is good or bad? Does any of this sound familiar? The answers to these and all of your questions are coming soon, so be patient.

Some Answers: History

Santa Claus, or Saint Nicholas was born between 300 and 400 A.D. That would make him at least 1,600 years old.

St. Nicholas was the Bishop of a church in a place called Myra. It was then ruled by Greece, but is located in what is the country of Turkey today. He was born to a wealthy family. As a boy, his parents died, and he gave all of the money they left him to the poor.

This and other stories of Nicholas' generosity spread all over Europe. The Russian Orthodox Church, the Roman Catholic Church, and some protestant churches all recognized the kind works of Nicholas. Inspired by his selflessness, people soon began to give gifts to one another to honor him on his feast day—December 6. Eventually the custom became associated with Christmas. He is called different things in different countries. Father Christmas, Papa Noel, Babbo Natale, La Pére Noël. Why our own Santa Claus is a mispronunciation of the Dutch Sinterklass, which itself is a blending of Sint Nicolaas (Saint Nicholas).

Most of what we know about Santa Claus today comes from his description in the poem "A Visit from St. Nick," also known as "The Night Before Christmas" by Clement Clarke Moore. This was first published in the Troy, New York Sentinel on December 23, 1823. The story is filled with reminders of Bishop Nicholas—his outfit symbolizes the red hat and robe worn by a bishop. Nicholas often lectured children on being good, which could be why Santa has that list he always checks twice. Even the tradition of leaving gifts in stockings originated with Nicholas throwing a bag of gold into a family's window, and it, by chance, landing in a stocking that was drying by the fire.

Around 1841, Santa began his tradition of showing up at department stores and malls when J.W. Parkinson, a Philadelphia merchant suggested that Santa climb the chimney outside his shop.

In 1868, Thomas Nast, a Harpers Weekly illustrator began drawing his image of St. Nick with whiskers, and established him as a toymaker residing at the North Pole.

In the 1930"s, Coca Cola hired the chubby saint to help boost sales during the winter. They called on an illustrator named Haddon Sundblom whose drawings gave us the image of Saint Nicholas that we have today.

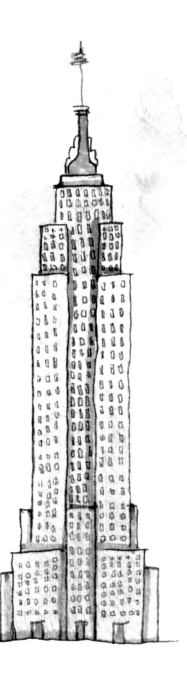

Some More Answers: Math

Today, Santa has to visit about 330 million children on Christmas Eve. Each home has, on average, 3 or 4 kids, so that works out to about 94 million houses. By-the-way, a glass of milk at every stop means Santa would have to drink 4,329,000 gallons of the stuff.

Because it is not night at the same time all over the world, he has 31 hours to deliver gifts. That means he must fly at 650 miles per second. Even when someone is driving a car a little too fast, they probably never reach more than 70 miles per HOUR.

Gifts for 330 million children weigh about 350,000 tons. This is about the weight of the Empire State Building!

I am guessing that by now, you are thinking that a jolly old man in a red suit cannot do all of the things you once believed he could. But that does not mean that Santa Claus is not real. Of all the people born over 1,000 years ago, how many of their names do you know? Had Saint Nicholas taken his inheritance and lived out his life as a wealthy man, you wouldn't know his name either. But the spirit of this bishop and his message of generosity live on in the hearts of parents around the world.

As a child of three, four or five, the magic of our modern version of St. Nicholas was a fun story that you could understand. But now you are old enough to comprehend a new story—one which is even more magical and beautiful. You should be excited, for now you get to be part of the story.

You can take the spirit of an orphan boy from Turkey into your heart and share it with others—your younger brothers, sisters, cousins, friends and neighbors, and one day with your own children. You will soon know that this feeling is more wonderful than waking up Christmas morning to find presents under the tree.

Every year there are countless tales of kindness and goodwill spread throughout the Christmas season. Christmas cheer is not only to be shared with children. I once experienced the joy of sharing the spirit of St. Nicholas with my 80 year-old grandmother, who, as a young girl, was too poor to receive a doll for Christmas. I searched antique stores until I found a doll that was made around the time she was five, and presented it to her that Christmas. She later recalled this as her very favorite memory.

Now, on Christmas Eve, I read *"The Night Before Christmas"* and the story of the Nativity to my children. I love being up late putting toys together and making boot prints with ash by the fireplace. There is not a moment all year which is more satisfying than when, after all the work is done, I can sit by the fire and enjoy the milk and cookies left by my children. I feel like Santa Claus because *I am* Santa Claus! When you help to make someone's life magical, you will believe in Santa Claus stronger than you ever did when you thought he was just a guy in a red suit. It is real, and one day you will understand that living on in the hearts of millions for over a thousand years is much more spectacular than flying reindeer.

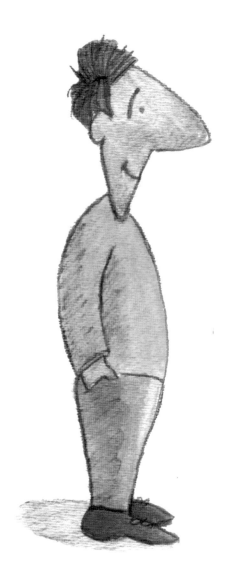

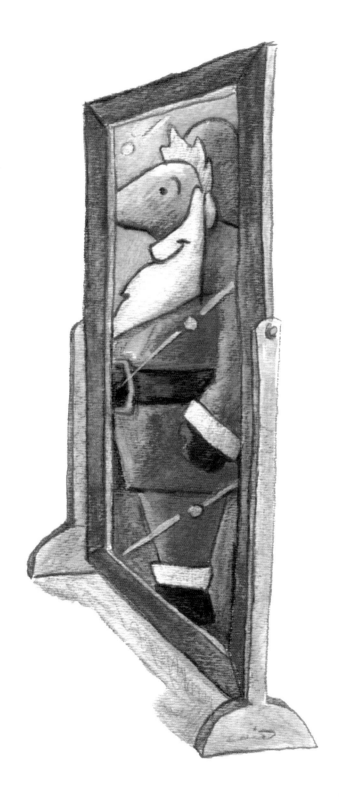

Made in the USA
Lexington, KY
10 December 2012